"Reflections" ---

... for sharing dreams

... all thoughts are originals of :~

       ... Brock Tully

illustrations :~

       ... Heidi Thompson

calligraphy :~

       ... Brock Tully

* printed on recycled paper.

Inspired by...
    those who believe, as i do,
that we 'all' have beautiful
hearts & it's when we lose
touch with our hearts that
we do the not so nice things
that we, too often, do.

Dedicated to...
    those who reach out &,
through their understanding,
support, & caring, give us
the strength to get back
in touch.

"... peace begins
    when we begin
        to see
    that peace begins
        within."

"... when i strive
        to live life
            to the fullest...
    i feel
        'full of life'
            while i'm living it."

"... it's important
that i love my work
so i can buy
a house & lot...
but what works
the best for me
is to have a 'home'
with lots of love."

"... i felt negative
         When i thought
      i was a 'Victim'...

but really
      i was only a Victim
   of negative thoughts."

"... i'm taking more risks &
    i've started going after my dreams,
        since i stopped
    Worrying about
        What others think,
            & stopped thinking
    others Would Worry."

"... by being honest,
    you may hurt my ego
            for a moment,
    but in a moment
            you'll have strengthened
    our trust."

"... i used to feel
                i needed a reward
        to feel good about
                what i 'did'...

        now i feel the reward
                is feeling good about
        what i'm 'doing'."

"... advice adds another voice
to my head
to confuse me ...
& gives me another person
to blame
when their advice
doesn't work."

"... future promises
often give me
a false sense of security...

as i'm sensing
what's false
in the moment,
i'm becoming securer."

"... i'm no longer dreaming about how
    i'd like to be living...
i'm now 'living the dreams',
    i used to long for."

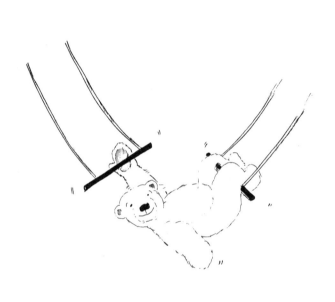

"... i like where i'm at
              now...
          because i'm in
              the 'now'
          ¿ that's where
              it's at."

"... i think subconsciously
    we create crises

                such as war
        to bring us together...
but when we have
            'us' & 'them',
    no one really wins...

as we become more conscious,
    we begin to see
            we can come together
        without these crises...
            & the only way
    we can win

                is to see
    we are 'one'."

. Why do we love that
         dogs, cats, & flowers
    are all different
             colors, kinds, & styles...

  & yet it's those very same qualities
          that seperate us
                 so much?"

"... you may not like
the way i look,
but i look
the way i'm like...

so would you like
to know me,
or would you like me
to know
that you only like me
for my looks?"

"... it's not changing places
that will make

me change...

it's the change
that takes place

in me...

... although a change of place
may help that change

in me
to take place."

"... when i think i need
                to belong,
       i often follow others...

When i follow my heart,
       i feel like i belong
regardless of others."

"--- i don't want you
        to be nice to me,
    'just' when you're afraid
            of me leaving---

i want you to be nice to me,
        because you feel
    it's the way you want to be,
        & then,
    i won't even think
            about leaving."

"... when i say
          i 'know' someone
          i often don't know
                    we're drifting apart...

when i know
          i never really 'know' someone,
                 it's exciting to know
                       there's always more
                   to get to know."

"... i can be hurt
                by others
        in 'all' ways
            except spiritually...

the 'only' way
    i can be hurt spiritually
            is by wanting
    to hurt others
            in 'any' way."

"... it's when i think
          i know everything,
     that i don't know
          i have the most to learn ...

     it's when i think
          i know all the answers,
     that i need to question
                    my thinking."

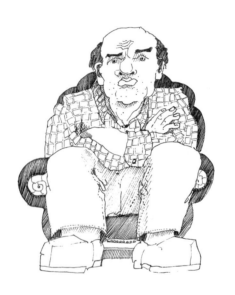

"--- some people 'seem to hate'...

i want to love
            those who 'seem to hate',
by seeing that
            they might 'seem to hate',
                not because they hate,
but because they're not happy
                with themselves,
        ¡ the way 'they're' living."

"... Why is it that
we can see someone
over & over again
in our home town
& never say hello ...

& yet, often,
if we see them
in another town,
we will run up to them
like they're
a long, lost friend?"

"... most often,
    my ego needs
            'to talk',
    & it hopes it finds
        a listener...
my heart loves
        'to listen',
    & it hears most
        when no one's
            talking."

"... i don't want to
go through 'the motions'
of life ...

i want to live life
with emotion."

"... When i bathe myself
        in the presence of people
                who nurture
        my self~esteem...

... i'm having
        an 'esteem bath.'" ☺

"... often,
    those who are sure
        there 'is' a God,
    seem more loving
    than those who think
        'they' know
            for sure
    who God is."

"... i'm done talking about
what i should
be doing ...
& i've started doing
what needs to be done
by doing away with
'should.'"

"... When we communicate,
we see that
our likenesses
are greater than
our differences...

When we don't communicate,
we're more likely
to 'only' see
our differences."

· so often
we strive to get
the trophies, marks, ¿ money,
hopefully to make ourselves
feel better
¿ maybe even
to impress others...
¿ yet when we 'pass on'
the ones who made
the greatest impressions
weren't those who cared about
what others thought,
but were those who were
the most thoughtful
¿ cared."

"... i feel more positive
                    & peaceful
when i put my energy
                        into doing
            what i believe in,
than when i go against
            what i don't ...

        --- & i smile more often too!"

"... if i take part
         in taking apart others
                         by gossiping...
     others will probably
                 gossip about me
       as soon as we're
                     apart."

"... some people's bodies
have left
this life...
i want my life
to embody
the beauty they've left."

"... When i thought
                the light
        Was at the end
                    of the tunnel,
        i got tunnel~Vision...

When i see
        that the light's Within,
there's no longer
                    any tunnels
            Visible".

"... i'd rather
          you be upset
        because i care about
                a lot of people ...
    than for a lot of people
              to be upset,
        because i'm not
                very caring."

"... through fear
          i can be taught
        & the more i'll know...
but
      when i'm motivated, i'm unafraid,
              & i'm excited
          to know more."

"... the people
who really are
ageless,
are those
who really don't
believe in age...

because they're too busy
being real."

"... i appreciate you
            working so much
so we can have
            a big, beautiful `house'...

but,

    i'd rather see you more
                in a little `home'
    because i think
                you're beautiful."

"... why is it that
            the ones
    who don't trust others
        are often
            the untrustworthy ones...

¿ the ones who trust
        know they can't trust
                            everyone,
        but every one
                they meet
        may be someone
                they can trust?"

"... our fear
       of allowing others
    to say
          what they feel,
  i feel,
     is way scarier
                than whatever
            they may have to say."

"... thankyou
for caring enough
to take the time
to show me
that we need
to take the time
to show that we care."

"... when i'm too concerned
          about personal gains,
     i don't feel
               as fulfilled
          in my heart & soul ...

When my sole concern
               is the hearts
     of all persons,
          i feel full again!"

"... a strength
            isn't 'acting'
        by putting on
                    a strong face...

    a strength
            is the action
        of facing
                our weaknesses."

"... 'you're' not bad
          because of
what you did ...

you're good,
          although what you 'did'
          was bad."

"... i'm not a human being
        spending a lot of time
    trying 'to become'
            spiritual ...

    i'm a spiritual being
        experiencing the trials
            of being human,
    for a short while."

"... it's not so important
                'where'
            i love to go
                    with you,
    as
        i love to be
                with you
        & go anywhere."

... distributed by Simon & Schuster
(Green Tiger Division)
1 (800) 223-2336 (U.S.)
General Publishing
(416) 445-3333 (Canada)

at the end of my other 'Reflection' books
i listed special books & movies. Again,
here, i suggest reading as much about
the teachings of Gandhi & Martin Luther
King as possible. (and don't forget
'Winnie-the-Pooh'!)

~ i would also like to highly recommend
a book called 'The Peace Pilgrim', named
after a woman who walked for 28 years
for world peace. Her book is only
available by writing & sending a donation
to ...   "Friends of Peace Pilgrim"
              43480 Cedar Ave.
              Hemet, California, 92344

with love
always,
Brock Tully